HEAVENLY

ANGELS UNAWARE

PAT ROGERS

Author's Tranquility Press
MARIETTA, GEORGIA

Copyright © 2022 by Pat Rogers

All rights reserved. No part of this publication may be reproduced, distributed, or transmitted in any form or by any means, including photocopying, recording, or other electronic or mechanical methods, without the prior written permission of the publisher, except in the case of brief quotations embodied in critical reviews and certain other noncommercial uses permitted by copyright law. For permission requests, write to the publisher, addressed "Attention: Permissions Coordinator," at the address below.

Pat Rogers /Author's Tranquility Press
2706 Station Club Drive SW
Marietta, GA 30060
www.authorstranquilitypress.com

Ordering Information:
Quantity sales. Special discounts are available on quantity purchases by corporations, associations, and others. For details, contact the "Special Sales Department" at the address above.

Heavenly: Angels Unaware / Pat Rogers
Paperback: 978-1-958179-32-1
eBook: 978-1-958179-33-8

Contents

DEDICATION 6
HEAVENLY 7
    CHAPTER TWO 12
    CHAPTER THREE 23
THE PAINTBOX 26
    CHAPTER TWO 29
    CHAPTER THREE 31
HE LIVES 36
SOMETIMES 38
ONCE UPON A TIME 40
FREEDOM FROM THE DARKNESS 41
THE HITCH HIKER 43
HOW BLESSED I AM 48
NOT GONE, JUST FORGOTTEN 49
THE ANGEL WITH THE JEEP 51
RESTING IN THE BOSOM OF THE LORD 54
HAVE YOU EVER HEARD GOD'S VOICE? 56
FOOT PRINTS IN THE SAND 57
WAS GOD THERE, THAT DAY? 59
OLD DOG AND ME 62
BY A ROCKY GARDEN WALL 65
ANGELICA 66
THE HUMMINGBIRDS 73

TWO THOUSAND YEARS TOO LATE	75
THE DAY THE ROSES CRIED	77
SEASONS	79
DAYBREAK	82
THE STORM	83
STARLIGHT	86
LORD, WE NEED RAIN	89
CROSSING JORDAN	91

DEDICATION

This book is dedicated to all those who look forward to the time when they will know the peace and joy through Heaven's Gate. I'm a woman, in her seventies who felt it, in my heart, to write it. It has short stories, poetry and songs, I've written. Where you see 'song' I have written the words but I don't know how to write music. Feel free to make up your own music. If you write the music, record and are **successful with it, please give me just a teeny, weeny, itty bit of credit for it. If you like to write, do it. Words are only a concept in the mind, until you share them.**

Blessings to you all, your friend in Christ

Pat Rogers

HEAVENLY
ANGELS UNAWARE

Cold!

I huddled in a doorway, torn coat on my back, worn shoes on my feet.

Hungry!

I couldn't remember when I'd last had something to eat. Then, I saw a little girl standing in the freshly falling snow, crying as if her heart was breaking. I went and knelt down beside her.

"What's the matter, Little One?" I asked.

"I'm cold and I'm lost and I can't find my Mommy." She sobbed.

I tucked her inside my ragged coat. "Where did you last see her?" I asked.

"At the grocery store. She went to get something for supper and I saw a little puppy. I tried to catch it, but it got away and now I'm lost and I can't find my way back." She began to cry harder.

"Shhh-h-h. There's no need to cry. I think I know right where she probably is." As I picked her up, she laid her head on my shoulder and put her arms around my neck. "God loves you, Jacob," she said.

How did she know my name? I didn't know her and I hadn't told her who I was, so how did she know my name?

I knew there was a little grocery just around the corner and about halfway down the street and she couldn't have run too far. I could see the little footprints that were slowly being covered with snow that led that way. I hugged her close, trying to keep her warm. Then, I could see the lights from the grocery and I carried her inside.

She ran to a woman standing by the counter, who scooped her up and held her close. "Where were you? I was so worried!" The child pointed toward me and said, "I was trying to catch a little puppy, but it got away and I got lost. I told him I couldn't find you, but he said he thought he knew where you might be, so he picked me up and brought me here. Isn't he wonderful, Momma?"

Her mother, with tears in her eyes, ran to me and hugged me tight. "Thank you, thank you!" she exclaimed. "Something terrible could have happened to her! Here, take this. You look like you could use something to eat."

She pressed a ten-dollar bill in my hand, but I didn't want to take it. I hadn't helped the child for money but because she needed me. When I protested, she smiled and said, "Please take it. You deserve it for your kindness." Then she picked up the child and headed toward the door. "God loves you, Jacob." She said as she went outside. How did she know my name? The child hadn't told her.

I bought some bread, bologna and milk and when I went to check out, the clerk smiled and put a package of doughnuts in the bag. "Enjoy," he said. I thanked him and went out the door.

Then, I saw an old man sitting on a bench under the street light. He was shivering because he didn't have a coat. I took mine off and wrapped it around him. "No! No!" he exclaimed. "I can't take your coat!"

I just smiled and said, "Don't worry, I'll get another one. Are you hungry?"

He looked up and then lowered his head as if he were embarrassed. Then, he nodded. I sat down beside him and asked if he'd like to give me a blessing. He raised his head and smiled, his eyes sparkling as if my simple question had made him very happy. We bowed our heads and he gave a short, simple thanks. Then, we sat and talked and shared the bread and bologna and milk. I didn't have any kind of cup, so we drank out of the carton. We laughed and joked, but it was starting to get dark, so I stood up to leave. "Do you have some place to stay?" I asked. "Yeah, I got a good place. You?"

"I've got a pretty good place, too." I didn't tell him it was a packing crate near a heat vent and I had a piece of old carpet to put over me. As I started to walk away, he said, "Here, you better take your coat."

"I'll be fine. My place is warm and you just have a shirt. It's not much, but you need it more than I do. Oh, and keep the rest of the food. I'll have breakfast at a place I know.

Take care of yourself." We shook hands and I turned to leave. That's when I heard three voices say, "God loves you, Jacob." I turned back and saw three figures dressed in white and softly glowing; a woman, a child and an elderly man. They came and put their arms around me and I felt loving warmth and a sense of peace. Then they stepped back and slowly faded away into the soft glow of light. As I stood completely astonished, another man dressed in white came toward me. His eyes were gentle and his smile so sweet. He held out his hands and I saw nail scars. I dropped to my knees, tears streaming down my face. "I know you. I know who you are!" I sobbed. He gently lifted me to my feet, smoothed back my hair and wiped the tears from my face.

"And I have known you from the day you were conceived. I was there when, as a small boy, you knelt and asked me into your heart. The angels sang with joy, that day. I watched you when you were in school and you helped others who had problems with their lessons. Then you stayed up half the night doing your own work. I was with you when you worked at your first job until the store closed and you were living on the street. I saw you work at any job you could find, no matter how little it paid, and then you gave most of what you had earned to those who had even less than you. You comforted the lonely, helped the sick and I saw when you found an injured dog that you took to a veterinarian and then worked, free to pay the bill. I know that your Bible is in the crate where you live and you pray every night, not for yourself but for those around you. Your faith and kindness have earned you a place in Heaven."

"Are you here to take me with you?"

"No, my child. You have an important mission here and you will bring many to me in my Heavenly home."

"When will it happen, Lord?"

He smiled and touched my cheek. "You will know when it comes to pass. Remember, I will always be with you."

He slowly faded away and I just stood there.

"Young man." a voice called. I turned and it was the store owner. When I walked over to him, he said. "I saw what happened out there. "The Bible speaks of 'entertaining Angels unaware." My name is John Casey and I'm getting too old to stock the top shelves. I need someone young, strong, and trustworthy. I've hired several different people, but they never seem to work out. I think you are just the person I need. Would you like a job? I can only pay minimum wage, but maybe later, I can pay more."

"You want to give me a job! I can't thank you enough, but you wouldn't have to pay that much. Would you let me take part of it out in food so I can help some of the people I know who are in need?"

"Son, you can spend what you earn any way you want to as long as it's legal."

CHAPTER TWO

Well, I'd worked there for five years stocking shelves and waiting on customers while Mr. Casey did the bookkeeping and ordering. The street was becoming more and more run down, so Mr. Casey bought the empty store next door and turned it into a soup kitchen. He finally got to do what he had always wanted. He loved to cook and he had only kept the grocery because it belonged to his parents. Now, he could cook to his heart's content. The street people, I knew, came in and he served them with a smile and a joke and they came to love him for it. The food was always good and plentiful and if someone wanted seconds, they were welcome to it.

His next project was to turn the upstairs into a shelter, but the men had to keep both themselves and the shelter clean and there was no smoking, drinking, or drugs allowed. He even took them to the second-hand store and bought them new clothes. Joe, Ray, Jim and Brad felt so good about themselves that they got jobs and their own apartments but they still came for Mr. Casey's cooking now and then.

He bought the vacant store on the other side of the building and turned it into a woman's shelter. A couple of them had children and they called Mr. Casey their

Grampapa. The women cleaned and dusted and polished until the place looked like new.

There was an alley between the soup kitchen and the grocery store, so his next project was a small chapel behind the grocery store where people could come and just sit to talk to the Lord.

I often sat there feeling the peace. I was there when Terry, one of the street people, came in and sat down. He seemed so sad I went to sit beside him. "How are things going?" I asked. He shook his head and said, "'bout as usual. I like this place. It feels good when I'm in here." "That's because the Lord is in this place." I said.

He just sat there and then he turned to me with tears in his eyes. "Is it really true that He forgives you even if you've done bad things? I have been on the street since I was a teen. Ain't got no education. I tried lots of times, but cain't get no job. I took things just to get by, but I never hurt nobody. I never smoked or did any kind of drugs but I stole a bottle, now and then, and got drunk, but it was only when things got real bad. Then, I heard 'bout gettin' forgiven for them things and I couldn't believe it was true. In here, though, I feel it, but I don't know how to get Him to forgive me."

I went to a table where we kept Bibles for those who wanted them. I handed it to him and said, "This is a Bible and if you read the New Testament, it will tell you anything you want to know about your Lord and Savior, Jesus Christ."

He didn't take the book. He just sat with his head bowed and twisting his hands together. Then he gave a sob. "I can't read. I never learned how. My teacher said I was too stupid to read. I can pick out a few letters, if they're big, but that's all."

I put my arm over his shoulders and said, "I'll read it for you and I'll teach you how to read. Would you like that?"

He looked up as if he didn't believe me. "You would? You really would? I'd like that a whole bunch, but when can I get forgiven and what do I have to do?"

I took him by the arm and led him to the little altar. "You kneel here, put your hands together, bow your head and pray."

"I never prayed before. I don't know what to say."

"Just tell Him what's in your heart and things you've done that you knew were wrong. You don't have to use fancy words, just talk to him the way you talk to me. And if things happened to you when you were younger, tell Him about that too. He will always listen. He will be the best friend you've ever known in your life. Then ask Him to take away all the bad things and heal your soul. He will always be with you."

I knelt beside him and prayed that he would find his way to the Lord. Then, I watched as he poured his heart out. He told about a childhood that made my heart break. He talked about being on the street, taking shelter wherever he could find it and giving it up because someone else needed it more. He told Jesus all the things he had done and, with tears running down the creases in his face, begged forgiveness. I found myself crying as he pleaded for the hope and peace only salvation can bring. At last, he stopped, laid his forehead against his hands and said, "Thank you, Jesus. I feel a whole lot better now. I promise I'm only gonna do good things from now on."

He stood up and we both wiped the tears from our eyes. "I want to learn lots more about Him. When can you start reading to me and teaching me how so I can read it by myself?"

"How about after I close the store, every evening. We'll come in here and I'll read to you and point out the words. But first, you said you could pick out some letters, so we'll see if you can pick out some of the ones I read."

"I can only pick out letters that are big, not little ones like in this book." He said.

"Let's try something. Can you pick out the words on the front of this book?" He hadn't taken the Bible from me, so I knew he hadn't seen the cover and I had a suspicion about why he had never learned to read.

He pulled the Bible up close to his face. "H-uh-o-lie Bib-lee." "This letter is a y but sometimes it's pronounced e." I said.

"With the first word, say the first letters together and then the last two letters and say them like an e. With this next word, say the first two letters together and the next two letters together, but don't say the last letter. Want to try again?"

He nodded and brought the book up close to his face again. "Ho-le-Bi-bl. Hole Bibl. I know it! I know it! Holy Bible! That's what it says, ain't it? I did it! I read it!"

"You sure did. Have you ever worn glasses or been to an eye doctor?"

"No, but I found some that had been thrown away. They were in pretty bad shape, but I could see a little better out of one eye 'cause they only had one glass. Then they got broke. But I ain't seen no doctor. I wish I could see better than I could get a job like I want."

"What kind of job do you want?"

"I want to learn to cook like Mr. Casey. I done a little bit, some times and I really like it but you got to know how to read the recipes and not just make things up." "Let's talk to Mr. Casey." I said. "He could probably use some help. You're strong and you could get heavy things down for him. I think he'll be glad to teach you about cooking. But, before I start teaching you how to read, I'm going to take you to see an eye doctor."

He was so excited, he danced around the chapel. "Can we go see Mr. Casey, now? I'll work real hard. I promise I will."

He was so overjoyed, he almost ran to the kitchen. Mr. Casey welcomed him, with a big grin and a twinkle in his eyes. "Guess what, Mr. Casey! Guess what! I was in the chapel 'cause I felt real sad. Then, Jacob came in and he showed me how to get Jesus to forgive me and he says he's going to read the Bible to me and teach me how to read. I got down on my knees and told Him all about me and now I feel real good. Then I told Jacob I'd like to learn to cook good as you." "So you want to learn to cook, do you? It can be hard work but, if you really try, it can make you very happy. You'll have to keep yourself really clean and we need to make you look like a cook." Mr. Casey took a chef's apron out of a drawer and tied it around him. "Now, Terry, you see those pots, scrub them clean and then we'll start cooking. Okay?"

Grinning from ear to ear, Terry hurried to do the job. Then, Mr. Casey turned to me. "Son, what you've been doing is making a big difference with these street people. I've never seen Terry look so happy."

"He was in the chapel wanting to be forgiven. Mr. Casey, he knelt and took the Lord. It was wonderful. He can't read and I told him I'd teach him, but I'm going to make an appointment to have his eyes examined. I don't think he can see really well and that may be why he has a reading problem.

The week after he had his eyes examined, I took him to get his glasses. When he put them on, it was as if a light bulb had lighted him up. He grabbed brochures and looked at them and then he went around looking at the names of the various types of glasses. "I can see the words, Jacob! I can see the words! Now you can teach me how to read".

Just about then, the Doctor came from the back. "What's all the excitement?" I told him about Terry's situation and how he'd been told he was too stupid to learn to read. An angry look came over his face. "I'll bet they never tried to find out what the problem was. A poor kid from a poor neighborhood and no one thinks he's worth helping. I was a poor kid, from a poor neighborhood, but I had the good fortune to have people who cared about me. That's how I became a Doctor. Terry, come here a minute. I have something to tell you." Terry went to him with a worried look on his face. "Terry, I want you to come and see me once a year. I'll check your eyes and if you need new glasses, you'll get them free. As long as I'm a Doctor, you'll be taken care of absolutely free. No one is ever going to tell you that you're too stupid to learn to read. No one! Not ever again!"

Tears ran down Terry's face as the Doctor put a hand on his shoulder. "Try hard to learn and make me proud." "I will! I sure will. I'm gonna learn to read a lot of things. Thanks so much. You'll be real proud of me!"

As we left, I looked back and the Doctor gave me a big grin and a thumbs up. I went to the book section and bought several children's books to give Terry a head start. He carried them proudly back to the shelter and showed them to the men sitting there. "I got glasses now and I can see the words. Jacob is gonna teach me how to read 'em and I'll be able to read the Bible all by myself. Then I can read lots of other books." The men whistled and whooped and gave Terry a thumb up. Then Bob put his arm around Terry's shoulder and said, "Sometimes Jacob is real busy so how about I help too? I like to read and, between the two of us, we could have you reading in no time." Terry turned to me. "Would that be okay, Jacob?" "I think it would be wonderful. When you have some free time from Mr. Casey, you could be studying." Just then, Mr. Casey came out of the kitchen. "What's all the hullabaloo?" he asked. When he found out, he gave Terry a slap on the back and said, "Wonderful! Absolutely wonderful but first let's get supper ready and everything cleaned up and then you can get to your books." Terry hustled into the kitchen and Mr. Casey came to me. "Do you really think he can learn to read?" "I'm positive. I think he's a lot smarter than people think he is."

In two months, he had finished with the children's books and was reading at a higher level. When I was working, Bob helped him and I was amazed at how fast he learned. He seemed to devour books. I never saw him without one in his hand. Then, every night, after I had closed the store, he was waiting for me in the chapel. I had started with the New Testament and he listened with rapt attention. Soon, I started letting him do the reading and he did remarkably well. He stumbled over an unfamiliar word now and then, but he never failed to ask what it was and what it meant. When he read about Jesus being baptized, I had to explain it to him and he decided he should be baptized, so we went to a church about three blocks down the street and talked to pastor Mark. "Glory, hallelujah, son! It would be my pleasure to baptize you. Next Sunday is when we do the baptisms. I only have one other person scheduled, but I'd like you to be first and tell about yourself and why you want to be baptized. I think you will be a true blessing to my congregation."

The next Sunday, we headed for the church and everyone who lived at the shelter went with us. Pastor Mark explained to Terry that, after he told about himself, he would go into the dressing room and change from his clothes into a white robe, walk up the steps to the baptismal and step into the water.

After the service had started, Terry was called up to the pulpit. Pastor Mark called for silence and then began to speak. "Folks, we have a very special young man with us today who wants to be baptized, but first, I want you to hear from him." He patted Terry on the shoulder and gave him a nod. I could see that Terry was nervous, so I signaled him to pray. He folded his hands and bowed his head for a couple of minutes and then looked up, all nervousness gone.

When he told about his life and how Salvation had changed him, I saw several tears throughout the congregation. "Jacob figured out why I couldn't read. I needed glasses. Now I can read the Bible, and other books, by myself. I never realized how much joy there is in being able to read. But, I haven't told Jacob, yet, that I want to go back to school and learn more so, I can graduate with a cap and gown like the other students. Then I want to go to cooking school."

Believe me, I cried like a baby. I was so proud of him. Pastor Mark came to the pulpit with tears in his eyes also. "Son, go get ready for your baptism." In a few minutes, Terry walked up the steps and into the water. There was a hush in the room. Pastor Mark put his hand on Terry's back and, with a handkerchief, in the other hand said, "Terry Brentwood, in the name of the Father and the Son and the Holy Ghost, I baptize you." Then he lowered him into the water. When he brought him back up, Terry raised his hands and said, "Thank you for all your blessings, Jesus. I love you."

There was applause and shouts of joy as the congregation all got to their feet. Then another wonderful thing happened; Bob, Cody, Crystal and her fourteen-year-old daughter Becky went and knelt at the altar. Wet robe and all, Terry went and wrapped his arms around them and prayed with them. After the service, everyone congratulated him and told him how proud they were of him. I've never seen so many hugs and handshakes and kisses, in my life.

He kept reading the New Testament and when he came to how Jesus was tormented and the suffering he endured before the crucifixion, he jumped to his feet and began to shout. "They shouldn't have done it! He was a good man! He helped people, so why would they want to do him that way? They killed him! It wasn't right!" I took him back into the Bible and we read again where Jesus told his disciples how he would be betrayed and that there would come a time when he must leave them and that he would suffer death to save the world from sin but that in three days he would return from the grave and be with them before he arose into Heaven. "So they killed Him but He came back" Terry said. "Death couldn't keep Him, so now he lives forever. Hallelujah, hallelujah!" "That's right. He lives forever."

CHAPTER THREE

It was summer so there was no school, but we talked to a local junior college and after testing showed how intelligent Terry was, they agreed to admit him and start him as a sophomore. That meant, if he kept his grades up, he would graduate in two years. He was so excited; he bought a calendar and marked off each day. He was always singing or whistling or humming when he wasn't working or reading.

Then, one morning, I came out to open the store and found him up on a ladder, hanging pots of flowers on the corners of the building. "What are you doing, Terry?" I asked.

'This place is too dull. It needs to be prettier. I'm going to hang flowers on all three buildings."

That was the beginning of change. When he wasn't busy with work or studying, he swept the sidewalks and washed windows in every store, whether anyone owned them or not. Gradually, people began to move into the vacant stores. Crystal and Becky opened a flower shop. Toby opened a shelter for homeless animals and got them adopted. A deli opened and more stores began to come in. Those who lived in the shelter cleaned up the park across the street and took it upon themselves to monitor it so kids could play safely. We had eight people come to the Lord and change their lives. Three of them went on to good jobs and their own apartments. One got married and moved out of town.

The last I heard, they had a brand new baby boy they named Terry Joe. Clyde is a minister in a little church in Idaho. He's also planning marriage. The other three went back to get their GED. When the Lord said I would bring people to Him, He knew that helping Terry would be the stimulus.

Many of the homeless, who came to the shelter, went on to make good lives for themselves and others went back to the streets.

Two years after Terry went back to school, he stood there in his cap and gown and when he was handed his diploma and a scholarship for two years at a cooking school, he positively glowed and when he showed it to Mr. Casey, they both cried.

Mr. Casey passed away recently and we all grieved, but we knew he was in a better place. He was a good, Christian man and we all loved him. In his will, he left the store to me, the soup kitchen went to Terry and he turned it into a pleasant little restaurant with excellent food.

People from all around the block ate there and anyone who needed a meal was happily served. The women's shelter became a place where children, whatever their need, could come. Sometimes it was for a meal and they brought their hungry family along. Sometimes it was just to have someone to talk to about problems or help with homework.

When I talked to the Lord, I never imagined how things would turn out, but now I know what it's like to "entertain Angels unaware" and speak, face to face, with the Savior of my soul.

Blessed be my rock and my salvation.

THE PAINTBOX

It was one of those stormy autumn days when teachers wondered why they chose their profession because the kids couldn't go outside to play during recess. Mrs. West was about to go insane with all the chatter, giggling and silliness small children can come up with. Suddenly an idea popped into her head.

"Children, pay attention. I know you can't go out for recess, so we're going to make an art gallery." "What's a gallery?" one of them asked. "It's a place where people can go and look at beautiful pictures and statues and all kinds of things." "I know! I know!" One shouted, waving his hand in the air. "I went to one and they had dinosaur bones and bows and arrows and axes and all kinds of stuff like that. Will we have anything like that?"

As she passed out sheets of paper, she explained. "You will draw a picture and since you all have crayons or colored pencils and MaryAnn has a paint box, you can color your pictures. Then, at lunch, I'll tape them all to the wall and everyone can look at them and vote on the one they like best. The winner will get a prize." "What kind of prize?" "A sketch book and an extra-large box of colored pencils.

Excitement filled the room as the children got busy with their artwork. A prize for the best was just the incentive they needed. Mrs. West smiled at their busyness and when she picked the pictures up, she praised everyone. There were pictures of airplanes, rocket ships, boats, cars, monsters and everything their brains could think of. She looked puzzled when she saw Mary Ann's picture. It was a circle of people of every color, even green, gray and blue. "MaryAnn, I think this is a beautiful picture, but why are some of the people green, gray and blue?"

"I'm helping God show all the colors of the people." "You're helping God?" "Uh-huh. When God made the people, I think there were so many that he ran out of colors in His paint box, so he had to make more colors to finish them." "But, MaryAnn, no one has ever seen people those colors!" "That's 'cause they live where no one ever goes. Way, way back in the jungle, where everything is really green is where the green people live.

That's so they can hide when they're in danger. And way up in the tallest, tallest mountains is where I think the gray people live. The rocks are all gray and it's really cold so, I think they live in caves in the rocks." "But, if it's all big rocks, what do they eat and how do they stay warm?" "They catch small animals and, even in rocks, there are plants that are good to eat and, I think God taught them how to make fire and to take what they couldn't eat and burn it. And they take the skins from the animals and make clothes. God knows how to do things."

"What about the blue people?" "I think they live way out in the ocean." "Do you mean mermaids?" "'course not. Mermaids are make believe. I've heard of places, in the ocean, where the water is warm and I think that's where they live. Maybe a sailor saw one and thought it was a mermaid. They play with the dolphins and (with a giggle) maybe sometimes the whales give them piggy back rides. That would be real fun. Sometimes, they come out on the sand, but they don't stay long 'cause the sun is too hot for them." "Can they talk?" "Sure, just like the dolphins and whales and birds and other animals talk. We can't understand 'em but God can. He can understand everything." "Are you sure you want this to be your picture?" "Sure. You said we could do any picture we want and this is mine."

CHAPTER TWO

At lunch, Mrs. West taped the pictures to the wall and invited everyone to look at them and pick the one they liked the best. Some of the children made fun of MaryAnn's picture, but she just shrugged it off. Billy (who had a vivid imagination) really liked it and he sat down with her and they had a long and spirited talk. Of course, some of the children began teasing and calling Billy her boyfriend, but she didn't care. She liked Billy because he was so smart. Then, the announcement for the prize was made and Jimmy won for his picture of rocket ships blasting off for the moon.

"You should have won." Billy said. MaryAnn just smiled and said, "I'm glad he won. It was a great picture and he doesn't have a lot of things. Besides, maybe now he won't be so bashful. I kind of feel sorry for him 'cause he doesn't have many friends. Maybe his picture will make the other kids like him more. He's a real nice person." "Do you think I'm nice?" "I think you're real nice and you're smart, too." "It's my birthday Thursday and we're having a party. Would you like to come?" "I'd like that but I have to ask my parents first." She gave him a smile and a wave and headed back to her seat. He strutted off with a big smile, as if he had just won a huge prize. While the children were studying, Principal Barker came in and spoke to Mrs. West. "At recess, please send MaryAnn to my office." "Oh, I hope it isn't about her picture." "I think it's a wonderful piece of art and I want to talk to her about speaking at Friday's conference, with her parents' permission, of course."

When MaryAnn went into his office, she was a little nervous. "Well, hello, Mary Ann." "Hello, Mr. Barker. Am I in trouble?" "Oh, my no. I want to talk to you about your picture. I think it was wonderful and very imaginative. I have a big conference coming up on Friday. There will be a lot of people there and, with your parents' permission, I'd like to show them your picture and have you tell them about it." "But, it's little. How could they all see it?" "I'll have it put on the overhead projector. You are a very smart little girl with an excellent mind, and I'd like them to see that. Some people might not understand your picture but, when you tell them about it, I'm sure they will see how smart you are. Would it be all right if I talk to your parents about it?" "Sure. Maybe my picture will make people think a little harder."

That night, she showed the picture to her parents. Her Dad studied it and then gave a nod. "You know," he said, "I think you're absolutely right. God made all the people, in this world, and he doesn't care one little bit what color they are. I hope your picture makes a lot of people think really hard and decide like you do, that color doesn't matter. It's what people have in their hearts that counts." He gave her a big hug. "You did a fine job, Love."

CHAPTER THREE

Friday came and MaryAnn wore her nicest Sunday dress. When they got to the parking lot at the school, there were so many cars they had difficulty finding a parking spot. In the auditorium, there were more people than MaryAnn had ever seen in her whole life.

Principal Barker came up to them and shook her parent's hands. "I saved seats for you right in the front row and MaryAnn you'll come with me up on the stage." He took her hand and led her up the stairs to a chair right beside the podium.

He rapped a gavel on the podium and then began to speak. "Ladies and Gentlemen, if everyone has gotten seated, we'll get this meeting going. But first, I have a special guest. Her name is MaryAnn and she's one of our students. Earlier this week, when it was so nasty, Mrs. West had the children create picture so we could have our very own art gallery. The picture that got the most votes received a prize. MaryAnn didn't win, but her picture impressed me so much that I wanted to share it with you, and when you've had a chance to look at it, she will tell you about it." He had the picture put on the overhead projector and waited for the audience's response. There was a lot of muttering and mumbling and some very puzzled looks. "Now, here's MaryAnn to tell you about her picture.

MaryAnn stood and walked to the edge of the stage. She was very nervous, but when she looked back at her father, he folded his hands and bowed his head, then looked up at her with a smile. She nodded and folded her hands to say a little prayer to comfort herself. Then she took the microphone and politely thanked the audience for coming. "I'm going to tell you about my picture and I hope you like it." She said. There were chuckles when she talked about the green, gray and blue people. Then, the audience quieted as if they were really listening and thinking about what she said. But one man, about three rows back, didn't seem too happy. Every time God was mentioned, his mouth tightened, and his cheeks began to turn red. The more God was mentioned, the tighter his mouth got and redder his face.

MaryAnn finished her talk, politely thanked everyone, and, giving a dainty little curtsey, turned to walk back to her chair.

Suddenly the red-faced man leaped to his feet and began shouting angrily. "Is this what they're teaching in school these days? About God and Him making the world and the people that are all kinds of colors? Ridiculous! There are rules about what can be taught in school!"

When MaryAnn heard the shouting of the man, she turned around, put her hands on her hips, and went back to the front of the stage. Taking the microphone, she said, "Excuse me! Excuse me, sir! The school didn't teach me anything about God and Jesus. I learned it in Sunday school. We learn lots of things in Sunday school and one of them is to be polite and not shout at people. If I acted like you, my Mom would give me a good whack on my bottom to teach me how to behave."

Suddenly there was a loud "Kerwhack!" The man grabbed the seat of his pants and glared down at the elderly woman sitting beside him. "What did you do that for?" "Because you deserved it." "I have a right to express my opinion and I think what that kid says is nonsense, talking about God and Him making people! It's pure nonsense. There are rules about teaching religion in schools!" There was another "Kerwhack." "Timothy James, sit down and shut up. That child makes more sense than you ever have. I should have taken you to Sunday school when you were little. Maybe you would have learned some manners." The man pushed and shoved his way from the seats, not caring whether or not he stepped on toes. Then he stomped angrily up the aisle and out the door.

'I'm sorry I made him mad, but I wish they taught about God and Jesus in school. Maybe people wouldn't be so mean. Maybe the bigger kids would stop bullying the little ones and the smarter kids would help the ones that weren't as smart."

The entire auditorium was on their feet, whistling and applauding. Someone shouted, "She's right. They should teach about God and Jesus in school. When I went to school, we said the Pledge of Allegiance and we blessed our food when we went to lunch." "Yeah!" came another voice. "We did that until, one day, a woman who didn't even live here, decided we shouldn't and she took it to the Supreme Court and look where we are now!" There were comments all over the auditorium until Timothy James' mother stood up. "I'm sure most of you know me. My name is Daisy Meriwether and I am Timothy James' mother. He used to be a pleasant boy until he grew up and started earning money. The more he got, the worse he became until he decided he could treat people any way he wanted. The Supreme Court has taken away our freedom of speech and a lot of other freedoms, but it can't take away my right to have religious pictures in my home." She turned to MaryAnn. "My dear, I want to buy your picture and hang it in my living room so people can see it. I'll tell them your story and, if my son lays so much as a finger on that picture, I'll get myself a switch and warm his britches until he can't sit down. Laughter rang, through the auditorium. I'm sorry you didn't win the prize, it's such a marvelous picture." "I'm glad Jimmy won. His family is poor and I know they were proud of him. He wants to be an electronics designer but unless he gets a scholarship, he won't be able to. He's real smart and real nice." "What do you want to be?" "I want to be a nurse that takes care of babies." "My dear, I'm a wealthy woman and I'm going to see that you and Jimmy have whatever it takes for the two of you to be able to study whatever you want. And, in my will, I'll donate your picture to the museum with a book that tells your story. I'll also donate enough money to be sure it stays there long after I've left this world."

With tears in her eyes, MaryAnn ran down the steps, eased herself through the seats and threw her arms around Mrs. Meriwether. "Thank you so much. You are a wonderful lady" "And you are a wonderful child. I want you to come to my home, to see your picture and bring Jimmy with you. I think we are going to become good friends and I wouldn't be surprised if you became our first lady president."

MaryAnn and Jimmy often visited Mrs. Meriwether and filled a lonely spot she had in her heart. She, in turn, began going to church with MaryAnn and her parents. She found an even greater friend when she knelt at the altar and accepted salvation. Her son rejected her newfound joy, but with MaryAnn, Jimmy and Jesus, she had all the peace and joy she needed.

From the mouths of babes comes joy and truth and from their hearts comes love and peace.

HE LIVES
A song I wrote

He is my rock. He's my foundation. He is my shelter from the storm. He is the fortress that protects me when the world will do me harm.

He picks me up when I have fallen. He wipes the tears from my eyes.

> My Lord, my God, my blessed Savior,
> For me to live, He had to die.

They took him up on Golgotha and laid his cross down on the stone.

They hammered nails into his body and with each nail I heard his groan.

He holds me close when I am grieving. He comforts me when I cry.

> My Lord, my God, my blessed Savior,
> For me to live, He had to die.

They raised the cross so all could see him, a crown of thorns upon his head.

The blood ran down like crimson raindrops, but he forgave what they did.

Down on my knees, I wept and trembled. I couldn't bear what they had done.

> My Lord, my God, my blessed Savior,
> For me to live, He had to die.

The thunder roared. The heavens darkened. The people ran away in fear.

But his mother knelt before him and she shed bitter tears.

I couldn't stay, my heart was broken. I stumbled down the rocky trail.

> My Lord, my God, my blessed Savior,
> For me to live he had to die.

They wrapped his body in white linen and laid him in a borrowed tomb

But in three days, the tomb was empty. He arose like he said he would.

My Savior lives just like he said. My Savior lives just like he said.

> My Savior lives, death could not hold him.
> My Savior lives just like he said.
> He lives just like he said.

SOMETIMES

Sometimes when life's storms and shadows deepen and darkness fills my heart with doubt and fear, I call upon the name of my Dear Savior to find that he is always near.

Sometimes when the road stretches before me so long that I can't see around the bend, I reach out for the hand of my Dear Savior; I know that He will lead me to the end.

He takes my hand. He leads me on; o'er shifting sand to the rock deep and strong. He is my path, my strength, my way. He is my guide, there by my side; He's with me to stay.

Sometimes when this world and all its pleasures are more than my poor trembling heart can bear, I cry out for the strength of my Dear Savior; I know that I will always find Him near.

Sometimes when there's darkness all around me and I feel that it will never go away, I cry out for the help of my Dear Savior because I know He will bring the light of day.

He takes my hand. He leads me on; o'er shifting sand to the rock deep and strong. He is my path, my strength, my way. He is my guide, there by my side; He's with me to stay.

Sometimes when my heart is filled with laughter and beauty in everything I see, I up look to the face of my Dear savior and know that He is always there with me.

Sometimes when the joy of Jesus fills me, I sing. I dance. I raise my hands to pray because I know He's always there beside me. He leads me through the burdens of my day.

He takes my hand. He leads me on; o'er shifting sand to the rock deep and strong. He is my path, my strength, my way. He is my guide, there by my side; he's with me to stay.

Reach for His hand, He's always there.

ONCE UPON A TIME
A song

Once upon a time, it seems like yesterday; I was deep in sin, shadows filled my day. Then a gentle voice said, "Child, take my hand. Walk with me awhile. You know I understand. Open up your heart and let me come inside." But, I was so afraid, I turned away to hide.

Then that gentle voice said, "Child, have no fear. With me in your heart, you'll know you'll I'm always near."

"Jesus, is that you? They say you're not real. How can I believe in what my heart can't feel?"

Then a gentle touch swept across my face and I knew that touch was God's own saving grace.

Now my heart can sing. Now my soul can soar, on the wings of grace, through Heaven's open door. There, I'll walk those streets of purest, purest gold until, upon his throne, my Savior I'll behold. Then He'll smile at me and take me to his side and he'll say, "Dear child, with me you will abide in this blessed place, by the crystal sea, safe here in my arms for all eternity.

Joy and peace is found only in salvation and prayer.

FREEDOM FROM THE DARKNESS

Traveling through the darkness of life's highway, shadows reaching for me, left and right. Voices whispering, "Come and join the party. You will find such pleasures here inside."

Will there be no end to all this darkness? Will the shadows drag me to my doom? The voices are becoming ever louder saying they will take away my gloom.

I am so afraid of all this darkness. Will there never be a ray of light? Will I walk this highway forever, always walking through the darkest night?

Still, I keep on walking in the darkness, wondering if my life will ever change. Shadows growing stronger, ever stronger. The voices making promises again.

Then, ahead, I see the faintest glimmer. It grows brighter as I walk along. Shadows try to drag me back to darkness. The voices say to leave that light alone.

The light keeps growing brighter, ever brighter. The voices say you must not go inside, for if you do, you will lose what we have given, prestige, fame, pleasure, wealth, and pride.

Then, another voice so sweet and tender says, "I will take you there, into the light." Shadows growing dimmer, ever dimmer, voices fading back into the night.

Then I feel a hand upon my shoulder. I turn and see a man all dressed in white. He smiles and fills my heart with such great gladness. His smile has cast the darkness from my sight.

I know, someplace before, I've seen his image. A picture hanging somewhere on a wall. And then I know who's standing there before me; Jesus Christ, the Savior of us all.

Now, I know darkness was my sinning, the shadows Satan's way to drag me down, and the voices were the sound of my temptation. But now, by Jesus' love, they're not around.

Jesus Christ, my sweet and loving Savior, died upon the cross to ransom me. But the grave could never hold him. In three days, he rose to set me free.

Cleansed, I know I'll walk with him forever by the waters of the crystal sea. He will place his loving arms around me and hold me safe for all eternity.

THE HITCH HIKER

I was taking a load of auto parts to a store in Denver, and the rest to a pet store, in Cheyenne. As always, my best friend was in the other seat; my Bible. As I cruised along, I saw an old man walking down the side of the road. He was skinny and bent, wearing a white shirt, faded jeans, and scruffy sneakers. As he walked, he stumbled now and then.

I wondered why an old fella, like him would be walking along the road. I hadn't seen a car in miles, so it couldn't be car trouble. Maybe he was just one of those who liked to walk for exercise. Nah! He was too old, and it was too hot.

I know! I know! Everyone says not to pick up hitchhikers but unless he had a pistol in his pocket, I figured he was too old to do me any harm.

As I pulled up closer to him, he turned, smiled, and stuck his hand out to thumb a ride. I pulled far enough ahead to get off the road and, in my side mirror, saw him shuffle up to the cab and open the door. "Need a hand getting inside." "Nope, I'll make it just fine. Not too many folks will pick up a hitchhiker these days. Guess they figure it's too dangerous and they're probably right. Truckers, though are more prone to help. I see you've got your helper with you." He said when he picked up my Bible. "How long you been carryin' it?" "Since I was a kid in

Sunday school." "You read it?" "Every day." "You know, if everybody carried a Bible and read it, the world would be a whole lot better place." He stuck his hand out to shake mine. "Name's Gabriel. Yours?" "Josiah, but my friends all call me Joe." "I knew a man named Josiah, but that's been a long time ago. He was a fine man, a Godly man." "How far are you going, Gabriel?" "Oh, just down the road a piece. I'll let you know when we get there." As we drove along, we talked and laughed. He told me about some of the people he'd met and I told him about mine. Somehow having him there made me feel better. I'd had some bad news and until I picked him up, it was all I could think about, and it was as if, every time I looked at him, he seemed younger. I figured it was just my imagination.

We rode along, in silence, for a while and then Gabriel turned to me and said, "You've got some troubles, don't ya, son?" "I guess everybody has troubles some time or another." "But not like this. Tell me about it. Sometimes talking helps but first, where are you heading?" I choked back tears. "To the hospital, in Cheyenne. Annie and I have been married thirty-two years; we have three kids and two grandkids. Benny, the youngest grandkid, was riding his bike and was hit by a drunk driver. He has some broken bones and he's been in a coma for three days. Annie called me, but I was too far away to get there any sooner. I had her call the stores where I had deliveries and let them know what happened. They said not to worry, they would send trucks to pick up their supplies and they would pray for Benny." Tears ran down my face and I could hardly see, but Gabriel patted me on the shoulder and said, "Don't worry about Benny. He's had hundreds of people praying for him, including your prayers, and, by the way, he just woke up and he wants some chocolate ice cream and a hotdog with mustard and catsup on it. Oh, and he just decided he wants pickles on it, too." "What? How do you know what he wants?" I looked over at Gabriel and almost wrecked the truck. There no longer was an old man in the other seat, but a young man with blond hair that hung to his shoulders and he wasn't wearing a white shirt, ratty jeans and scuffed sneakers, but a white robe and he seemed to glow. "Gabriel! Of course, you're the Angel Gabriel. Why didn't you tell me before?" "Because you needed to get the fear and worry out of your system. You needed to talk about it because you felt responsible for not being there when it happened. That's how parents and grandparents are. If you were halfway around the world and something happened, you would feel responsible because you weren't there to prevent it. Just around the hill is where you need to stop." "Stop! I can't stop. I have to get to Cheyenne!" "First, you have a job to do."

As I rounded the curve, I saw a car lying almost on its side in a ditch. I hit the brakes, jumped out of the truck and ran to the car. A young man came around the car, waving his arms.

"Help! My wife's having a baby and we don't know what to do! I ran back to the truck. "Don't leave us, please. We need help!" "Don't worry, I'm going to call for the police and paramedics. It won't take long for them to get here. Then I'll come back and we'll try to level the car as much as possible and if the baby comes before they get here, I watched all three of my kids being born, so I think I can handle it. Just don't panic." "Gabriel, would you put out some flares, so nobody runs into us?" He smiled and nodded. I climbed into the back seat and smiled at the young woman. "Hi, I'm Josiah. How are you doing?" "It hurts!" "Sure it does, but that comes with having a baby. Your husband is in such a panic you'd think he was the one having this baby. We'll have to get your panties off, so the baby has room to come." "I don't have any on 'cause I knew it was time. That's why we were heading for Cheyenne. Then, the tire blew and we went in the ditch. I'm so scared. What if my baby got hurt?" "Don't worry. Everything is going to be fine. In fact, it's crowning. Now, you need to ease up on pushing." I pulled my jacket off to catch the baby in. "The head's out. Don't push until I make sure the umbilical cord isn't around its neck. It's all clear and the baby has turned. Now, you need to push hard, so we get the shoulders out." She grimaced and pushed as hard as she could. Suddenly, as if he had been greased, a baby boy slid out into the jacket and gave a good, healthy cry. I wrapped him up and handed him to her. Then we heard the emergency people arrived. "The EMTs are here and they'll cut the cord and get you to the hospital" "What did you say your name is?" she asked. "Josiah." "And the other man?" I looked back, turned and smiled. His name is Gabriel." "I like that." She said as the medics were tending to her, "I'm going to name my baby boy Josiah Gabriel Johnson." As soon as they got her in the ambulance, they took off, leaving her husband behind. I guess they forgot all about him. Waving his arms, he yelled, "Hey! What about me? You forgot me!" I took him by the arm and led him to the truck. "Get in and I'll take you to the hospital. I've got a grandson there I need to see. By the way, what's your name?" "Dave." He said as he climbed in and buckled up, but Gabriel just stood there. "Hey, are you coming?" "No, I've got something to tend to down the other way. Take care and tell Benny hello for me. He shut the door, crossed the road and headed the other way. As he walked, he slowly aged and his clothes turned back to the white shirt, bedraggled jeans and scuffed sneakers. Dave watched him, his mouth gapped open. "What in the world! He changed!" "That's because he's an Angel." "You mean like in this?" he said as he picked up my Bible. "That's right." "Just think, my boy is named after a truck driver and an Angel. Bet no one else can say that." We followed the ambulance to the hospital and, after bidding each other goodbye, headed our own way. He went to see his wife and new baby and me to my wife and my grandson.

When you meet a stranger, you may find you're talking to an Angel.

HOW BLESSED I AM

Gracious Lord, hold my hand. I'm standing here on shifting sand. Lead me to that Promised Land. Gracious Lord, hold my hand.

Gentle Lord, wipe the tears that I've shed throughout the years.

For the ones I've held so dear. Gentle Lord, wipe my tears. Lord, you died on Calvary's tree. Your blood was shed to ransom me.

But you rose to live again and you took away my sin.

Precious Lord, I'm not alone. Through that gate, you led me home; never more will I roam. Precious Lord, I'm not alone. Wondrous Lord, I am blessed in this place of happiness. Here, I'll find sweet peace and rest, Wondrous Lord, I am blessed. Lord, you died on Calvary's tree. Your blood was shed to ransom me.

But you rose to live again and you took away my sin.

Blessed be the name of my Lord and Savior. Hallelujah. Amen.

NOT GONE, JUST FORGOTTEN

I saw the house in a shadowed forest glen; old and frail, its porch sagging; its windows, like blind eyes, dimmed by the passing years. Weeds choked the yard and a vine climbed the wall to the chimney with one fading blossom, like flowers in an old woman's hair.

It saddened me to see that old house; not gone, just forgotten. But then, like the shadow of a dream, it changed. Faintly, like an old and faded film, I saw chickens pecking in the yard while children, and one small dog, played a wondrous game of hide and seek. Momma, hanging clothes on the line, smiled and giving into the joyous pleas, joined the game, leaving just enough skirt showing to be found.

Then, I saw a man walking down the lane toward the house, greeted by laughing children. He hugged each one and then, arm around his wife, disappeared inside.

Your walls were white, your windows gleamed and flowers decked your porch, but time has taken all that away and now you're all alone.

Do you dream of the old house, of the days gone by when laughter filled the air? Do you dream of all the happy times that are no longer there? Do you dream of Thanksgiving when family, friends and neighbors sat around the table, held hands and thanked The Lord for the bounty set before them and Christmas time when snow fell, like thistle down, and they decorated the tree with a beautiful Angel at the very top?

Do you dream about the family that once made you their home; how they would sit at the kitchen table and bless the food before them? At night, the Dad would sit and read to them from the Bible, and then, kneeling with the children to say their prayers, he'd tuck them in and kiss them good night. But, one by one, they went their way and left you all alone?

How long have you dreamed, old house, that one day they'd return? But time has passed and years have gone and only shadows come.

It's sad to see you waiting there, in this shadowed glen, and know time will take its toll. You're not gone, just forgotten.

Remember the past for it is in remembering that we build our future.

THE ANGEL WITH THE JEEP
A true story

My brother had gotten into some minor trouble and had to spend six months at a work camp in the Colorado Mountains, and my sister-in-law, her little daughter and I would go see him about once a month.

We'd pack a lunch and head into the beauty of the mountains. It was a wonderful trip. There were lodge pole pine, fir, aspen and wild flowers to please the eye. But, on one trip, things weren't so beautiful.

It was one of those early winter days in Colorado, when the snow falls like goose down and, because the streets are warm, melts fairly quickly.

But snow fall on the flat lands can be a whole lot different than snow in the mountains.

I'll never understand why my sister-in-law wanted to make the trip that day, but I wasn't going to let her go alone, so we got ready and headed out.

The foothills had just a dusting of snow so it seemed that we'd probably have no problem with our trip.

It was still beautiful. The aspen had turned gold and shimmered in the breeze. I relaxed and just sat back to enjoy the view. But, as we got further into the mountains, things began to change. It began to snow; slowly at first but then it began to come down heavier and it was beginning to stick on the road. I suggested we turn and go back home, but I wasn't driving, so my suggestion wasn't taken. We traveled on and the clouds got darker and the snow got heavier. As we traveled higher, the roads began to glaze over and we had to creep along to stay in control.

We went over a fairly small hill, but the way up the next hill was a lot steeper. My sister-in-law gave the engine a little more gas, hoping to make it to the top, but we slid into the middle of the road.

She eased back into our lane and tried again, but we slid sideways again. She tried again, but it was no use. This time, the wheels just spun. Then a car came over the top of the hill and slid into the ditch of the other lane.

There we sat, wondering what to do next. Then, we saw a semi top the hill, horn blaring, lights flashing. I figured we were all probably going to die. The truck driver couldn't brake because he would have jack knifed with the trailer slamming into us and the cab hitting the car in the ditch.

Suddenly, we were back in our lane. The truck flew past us and the people in the ditch made it out and went on their way.

We just sat there, shaking with shock. Then a man in a plaid jacket tapped on the window.

"Do you ladies need a tow to the top of the hill?" he asked. We just nodded because we were too shaken to speak. He pulled his jeep ahead of us, hooked a chain to the car and pulled us up to the parking lot of a small service station that was closed, unhooked the chain, gave us a wave and was gone. There were no footprints, no tire tracks and no tail lights to show he had ever been there. Needless to say, we turned around and carefully headed back home. I will always believe he was an Angel sent by God to save our lives.

God sends Angels in times of need because He loves us.

RESTING IN THE BOSOM OF THE LORD
A song

When I was a sinner, I thought the world was my treasure.

I thought I'd find wealth. I thought I'd find fame and all the world had.

I ran with a rough crowd, ignoring my neighbor.

I didn't think anyone else was better than me.

Now I am resting, oh yes, I am resting,

In a pair of strong arms that will keep me from harm. I am resting, oh yes, I am resting, and I'm resting in the bosom of the Lord.

Then things started changing; I thought there's nothing for me.

I had a good home, shoes on my feet and a fine family.

But I had no contentment, no peace of mind.

Where ever I went, whatever I did, no joy could I find.

Now I am resting, oh yes, I am resting

In a pair of strong arms that will keep me from harm.

I am resting, oh yes I am resting.

I'm resting in the bosom of the Lord.

I stepped in a church to get out of the rain

And, there on the wall, an old wooden cross was calling my name.

I went to the altar, dropped down on my knees.

Lord for all that I've done, the way that I've, lived how can you love?

Now I am resting, oh yes I am resting,

In a pair of strong arms that will keep me from harm.

I am resting, Praise God I am resting.

I'm resting in the bosom of the Lord.

Yes, I'm resting in the bosom of the Lord.

HAVE YOU EVER HEARD GOD'S VOICE?

Have you ever heard God's voice? That's strange because I hear it every day. I hear it in the whisper of the breeze, in the trees, and at sunrise, in the song of birds as they wake and sing their morning song of praise. To me, it always sounds different in the morning than later in the day.

I hear it in the cry of a loon, the splash of frogs as they dive into the water and the sound of peeper frogs as they begin to sing; the sound of a brook as the water tumbles over stones; the crash of waves, on a sandy beach; the sound of water falling from some high place to splash into a pool below. I hear it in the cry of gulls, the song of whales

I hear it in the cry of a new born baby; the barking of a dog or the meowing of a cat. I hear it in the laughter of children playing some exciting game, the creak of a rope swing, the squeal of a child going down a sliding board.

There are so many ways to hear God's that I can't count them. They are as many as stars in the sky.

You say you haven't heard God's voice; maybe you just weren't listening.

Never stop listening and you will always hear God's voice.

FOOT PRINTS IN THE SAND
A Song

One day, while walking by the ocean, I turned
and saw my footprints in the sand.
I was lonely with no one beside me. My life
just hadn't gone the way I planned.
Then, I felt a hand upon my shoulder. I looked
and saw a man all dressed in white.
With nail scarred hands He turned me 'round
to see Him and then I knew exactly
Who He was.
My Lord, the Prince of peace.
He died, on Calvary's tree.
His blood was shed to wash away my sins and set me
free.
He said, "There's no reason to be lonely for
I am with you every night and day.

And when your path seems rough and lonely, that is when I'll show you the way. Come with me, let's walk beside the water and listen to the music of the sea

While overhead we'll watch the sea birds flying and I'll tell you about Eternity." We walked

And talked. He held my hand.

And when I looked,

I saw two sets of foot prints, in the sand. At last, I became so weary. He picked me up and held me to his breast.

I felt the gentle swaying of his footsteps. And then I closed my eyes in sweet, sweet rest. When I woke, there was no one beside me, just one set of footprints in the sand.

Where had He gone? He said He'd never leave

me. I wept because I felt so all alone.

Then, I felt a hand upon my shoulder.

I looked and He was right there by my side.

He said, "When you saw those single footprints,

My child that was when I carried you.

You'll never be alone because

I'll always carry you.

God is always there to carry you in your every need.

WAS GOD THERE, THAT DAY?

I had just moved into town and needed to find a church, so I decided to try the one just a couple of blocks down the street. It was big and grand, with magnificent stained glass windows and there were a lot of cars in the parking lot. So I decided it must be a fine church and I went in.

When I entered, there was no one to greet me and when I took a seat, people glanced around at me and turned away. It was as if I didn't exist. I looked around and marveled at the beauty of the decorations but somehow, I didn't feel the warmth I had always felt in church.

The pianist began to play and the choir came, all dressed in robes of white. They sang, with voices sweet, and then the preacher came. He greeted the congregation then bowed his head and opened with a prayer. "We're thankful for all those who are here today. We're thankful for the beautiful weather and the tithes that enable us to keep this church available for everyone. Amen."

Then he began his sermon. He preached about the blessing of having a church where everyone could worship and how fortunate they were that they had a place where they could gather together in fellowship.

As he continued with his sermon, I was shocked that he never once mentioned God's name.

When the sermon was over and everyone was leaving, I felt as if my heart was broken. God wasn't there that day.

The next week, I tried another church. It wasn't as big and grand and, when I went inside one person shook my hand. The pianist played and the choir came, dressed in what they had worn. They sang with voices sweet and then the preacher came. He laid his Bible on the podium and then began to preach without an opening prayer. He preached about the world and all the evils there. He preached about the churches where the Gospel was not taught. He talked about the homeless and panhandlers and said they could get a job if they tried. But I never heard him say the church should help those in need.

As I went back to my car, my eyes filled with tears. God wasn't there that day.

The next week, I tried another church. It was small and white and had a steeple. I saw people going in, so I thought I'd give it a try.

The minute I stepped in the door, people started shaking my hand. They smiled and introduced themselves and then they asked my name and said they were very glad I came.

The pianist started playing and then the choir came. They weren't dressed in fancy clothes but boy, how they could sing. When they had finished, that's when the preacher came. He laid his Bible on the podium and started with a prayer. "Dear Lord, we're thankful for all these wonderful people who came to be with You. We hope they will feel the love and care. You have for all of them. We ask your love for those who are sick and afflicted or having troubles that assail them. In Jesus name, we pray. Amen."

He preached from the Bible and called upon the name of God and Jesus and the Holy Spirit, not once or twice but many times and I felt the spirit filling that little church to the brim. When he had done, he prayed that everyone would get safely home and return for the evening service.

When I started to leave, people came to shake my hand again and said they hoped I would come back.

Walking to my car, my eyes filled with tears, but they were tears of joy. GOD WAS THERE THAT DAY! Hallelujah and amen.

> A church that is filled with love has
> people who are filled with love.

OLD DOG AND ME

Up in the mornin',
Sun's 'bout to rise.
Birds in the treetops
Old Dog's by my side.

One hand in my pocket,
Hot cup in the other.
Old Dog sits there yawnin'
Not a sound does he utter.
In the clear crystal dawnin'
Dog's head 'neath my hand,
We both stand there breathin'
The sweet smells of the land.
Wife's in the kitchen
Fixin' bacon and eggs,
Hot biscuits and gravy.
Old Dog sits and begs.

One last cup of coffee
And then out to work.
Gonna climb on that tractor.
Gonna turn that sweet earth.

Old Dog walks beside me
For a while, as a rule.
Then he finds him some shade,
He ain't nobody's fool.

He lies there and watches me
Go down field and up.
That's what he's been doin'
Since he was a pup.

When our day's work is over
It's back to the yard.
That Old Dog and me,
We're both plenty tired.

That night, by the fire,
Old Dog lies and dreams
That he's chasin' a rabbit
Over meadows and streams.

Sometimes we both wish
For what used to be.
Can't do what we used to
That Old Dog and me.

Next day is Sunday
So we head off to church.
Old Dog walks beside me
Kickin' up dirt.

He lies on the floor
By where Ma and I sit.
The folks there don't mind
That he comes, not a bit.

Later, I sit out there on the porch
Wife's in the kitchen, cookin' and singin'
The breeze shakes the leaves on the sycamore.
And sets the church bell ringin'.

Old Dog jumps up on the porch swing, with me
And then lays his head down for a nap.
After a while, he looks up at me
And then puts his head in my lap.

He just lays there, like he's a thinkin' "We ain't young like we used to be." I wonder if what he's thinkin' about Is it who'll go first, him or me?

I hope the Lord made a place
For old dogs and the critters folks love.
It seems it would be a real sad place
If there weren't no animals above.

Then, I get to thinkin'
What a fine thing it would be Just walkin' all over Heaven The Good Lord, Old Dog and me.

BY A ROCKY GARDEN WALL
A sonnet

This morning, by a rocky garden wall,
I see a bunch of rosebuds blushing red.
The sunbeams kiss each tiny nodding head
And sparkle through the dewdrops as they fall.

There, in the grass that grows so sweet and tall,
Is where a little mouse has made her bed.
And there she stays until her young are fed
Then rests them close and loves them one and all.

I know not why the wonders of this world
Have been revealed such a one as me;
Nor why God's love for me has been unfurled
Or why, within my hand He placed the key
That unlocks all the doors, of peace for me
And fills my heart with love for all mankind.

ANGELICA

Angelica was the littlest angel in Heaven. Her two favorite activities were flitting through the clouds and sitting atop the gate into Heaven and listening to the beautiful singing of the Heavenly choir. She was sitting on Heaven's gate, a smile on her face and a twinkle in her eyes when she felt someone sit down behind her. It was God. "You enjoy listening to the choir, don't you? He said. "Oh yes. I think I could sit here for all eternity just listening. They sound so beautiful. Look, one just left the choir and is heading for Earth. You must have sent that one on a mission." "Yes, a very important mission. You haven't been on a mission yet, have you?" "No, Father, but I know if there is a need, you will send me." "There is a need that only you can fulfill. There is a boy named Jeremy and he needs your help." "What does he need, Father." "You must find that out for yourself." He patted her on the head and sent her on her way.

When God sends an angel on a mission, they always know where they're going. She landed, on a sidewalk, dressed like any other little girl would be dressed. She looked around but didn't see anyone, but then a boy came around the house and sat down on a front step. He put his elbow on his knee, his chin in his hand and just sat there looking unhappy. She went up to him and said, "Hi, I'm Angelica. What's your name?"

He stood up, put his hands in his pockets and kicked at the step. "My name's Jeremy. I've never seen you before. Did you just move in?" "No, I'm just visiting for a while. You seem awfully upset about something. Maybe if you told me about it, you'd feel better. Talking does help, you know." He looked at her and then blurted out, "I want to be a superhero, okay! Everybody says that's silly and I'm too young!"

Angelica thought and thought until she had some idea what a superhero was. "Do you mean like those people who dress in funny clothes and fight with bad people?"

Jeremy gave the step a hard kick and hopped around, holding the toes he had just injured. Then he gave a sigh and said, "Those are just pretend. I want to be a real superhero like my uncle Max. He's a fireman." Angelica's eyes widen with astonishment. "You mean he's a man made of fire?" "No, silly, he goes where there's a fire and he helps put it out. Sometimes it's a house or a car or even trees in the forest. He rescues people, too. Once, he rescued a cat and her three babies. They took 'em back to the fire station and Uncle Max says it was the best rescue he ever made 'cause the cats keep the mice away, so they don't chew holes in the fire hoses. Real superheroes do good things for people. "You could do good things." "Like what? I can't put out fires or catch bad guys!" "Hmmm, let me think." She looked around and saw a yard that looked as if a storm had hit it. "Do you know who lives in the house across the street?" "Yeah, that's Mrs. Peterson. She's real nice and she makes the best chocolate chip cookies in the whole wide world and takes "em to the Old People's Home every week. She plays games with "em and plays the piano so she can get some of "em to dance. She says dancin' is good for the body and the heart."

Angelica walked down the sidewalk toward the house. "Her yard looks like no one has taken very good care of it." "She takes real good care of it, but there are some boys who come by here, sometimes, and they like to mess up her yard. They think it's fun and if she says something to them, they just laugh and make fun of her. They're real mean! Hey, I've got a good idea. Stay here, I need the wheelbarrow." In a few minutes, he was back with the wheelbarrow, a rake, clippers and a couple of sweat shirts. He tossed one to Angelica. "Here, put this on. It's too chilly to work outside without wearing something." Angelica slipped it on and was surprised at how good it felt. Never having been out of Heaven, she didn't realize what being chilly was.

Jeremy parked the wheelbarrow and got busy with the rake. "Pick up the twigs and put them in the wheelbarrow. Then we can cart them off." Angelica had never worked before but, once she got started, she found she rather liked it. They were working away when Mrs. Peterson stuck her head out the door. "What are you children doing? Are you the ones who have been messing up my yard?"

Jeremy looked up at her and grinned. "Hi, Mrs. Peterson. We're cleaning up this mess." "Why, Jeremy. I didn't know it was you. Thank you very much for your help. Who's your friend? I've never seen her before." "Her name is Angelica and she's just visiting." "Well. When you finish, come inside for some milk and chocolate chip cookies. I just made a fresh batch." "Sure thing, Ma'am. We'll do that. Won't we, Angelica?" "I guess. I've never had chocolate chip cookies before." "What! Where are you from? I thought everybody knew about chocolate chip cookies! You just wait. You're gonna love 'em."

They worked, laughing and singing, until the yard looked beautiful. "You know what; I'm going to mow her yard every week. She's so nice and it's hard for her to mow." Just then, Mrs. Peterson looked out the door. "Oh my, it looks beautiful. Come on in, you lovely children." They followed her and sat down at the kitchen table to glasses of cold milk and a plate of cookies. Angelica was amazed at the taste of cookies and milk. "Mrs. Peterson. Could I take a couple of these for my Father? He's never had chocolate chip cookies, either." "Why bless you child. I'll bag up some for both of you."

Jeremy gave a little shiver and said, "It's really chilly in here. Would you like me to turn up the thermostat, a little, for you?" "It wouldn't do any good, my dear. The furnace doesn't work very well and I can't afford to have it fixed. That's why I bundle up, when it gets a little cold outside. Will I see you in church, Sunday?" "You bet."

"You go to a place where you worship God, on Sunday?" Angelica. "Yeah, we have Sunday school and I like it. We learn all kinds of things about God and Jesus. You know what? Jesus was a Super Hero. He taught people to be nice to each other and He healed people who were blind or sick or couldn't walk.

Then, the big shots, like the priests and Rabbis made like He was bad and they beat him up and then nailed Him to a cross to kill Him but He forgave them for what they did. He died but He didn't stay dead. In three days, He came back to life. I guess that makes Him the very best Super Hero of all.

You know what, I'm gonna go to all the neighbors and the people at church and at school and collect things I can recycle so I can help Mrs. Peterson get her furnace fixed." "Want to help me collect stuff?" "Oh, yes. I think I would like that very much!" They covered the neighbor, collecting aluminum cans and bottles and anything else people were willing to give and, when Jeremy told why they were collecting, some even donated money. They all knew Mrs. Peterson but didn't realize what a hard time she was having.

As evening came, they lugged their collections back to Jeremy's garage. "Whew!" he exclaimed. "But I'm gonna keep it up until there's enough to get her furnace fixed. Tomorrow's Sunday. Want to go to church with me?"

"I'm sorry," Angelica said, but I have to leave this afternoon. I think you're going to be a Super Hero. You're well on your way, just keep it up and maybe more of your friends will want to be Super Heroes, too. Bye. It was really nice to know you." They waved goodbye to each other and Jeremy started to go in the door, but when he looked back, Angelica was gone.

In the twinkling of an eye, Angelica was sitting on Heaven's gate with God. She handed Him the bag of cookies. "Mrs. Peterson sent these for you. She's really a nice person." "I know." He said. "She makes good cookies, too. She will one day be in Heaven with us and not because she makes good cookies but because she has been born again."

They sat on the top of the gate and ate chocolate chip cookies while they listened to the angels sing. "Father, why does wanting to be a Super Hero help Jeremy to see the Light?"

"It's just the beginning. Being a Super Hero helps him learn to be kind and helpful. He has already given his heart to me but helping others makes him stronger in his faith. One day, he will become a fireman, like his uncle and he will feel even stronger in his belief."

Angelica thought for a minute, and then nodded her head. "I see, now. Will I help others sometime?"

"Indeed you will. In fact, I have a mission for you right now." "She smiled and when God told her what her mission was, she spread her wings and plunged happily toward Earth." God smiled because he knew she was going to be a very productive little angel.

On Earth, Jeremy continued his project and, impressed by his diligence, Harvey's Plumbing and Heating went to Mrs. Peterson's house and, in addition to installing a new furnace, they checked all her plumbing and replaced anything that needed it.

When Jeremy grew up, he became a firefighter and worked at it until his retirement. But he continued to collect recyclables for others in need. When the end of his earthly life came, he met Angelica and God at Heaven's gate. She ran to him, hands outstretched. "I'm so proud of you. You became a real Super Hero. God smiled and said, "You were always destined to be a Super Hero. Your faith and kindness helped many follow in your path. Welcome, my child."

The size of the Angel doesn't matter. It's what's in the heart.

THE HUMMINGBIRDS
A true story

The year was 2013. Mom went to be with God that February, much too soon for the hummingbirds to arrive.

She, and I, loved it when we knew they were on their way. I kept track on the computer map so we knew when to put out the feeders. Sometimes, it was a week or so too soon, but they always arrived. We had one feeder out front and we could watch them from the front window. The two on the deck, we could see from the kitchen.

Sometimes, a little male would sit on top of the feeder and watch intently just in case there were others trying to invade his territory.

During the spring, there was always magnolia, dogwood, and forsythia, in bloom, so they never failed to have a veritable banquet, but they always came back to the feeders.

One year, a little hummer crashed into the window and we were afraid it had broken its neck, but Mom went out and picked it up. She gently stroked its little back and, in a few minutes, it raised its head and looked up at her. It didn't seem afraid. It just sat there and, then with a flutter of its wings, flew away.

We often sat on the deck to watch them. Sometimes there were three or four at the feeder at the same time (usually females because they seemed to get along much better than the males). The males usually scrapped and chased the others away. Then, the males would begin their courting dance, trying to entice some cute little girl. Watching them was pure joy. In the fall, they would start heading south.

The fall Mom died, my little hummers were down to two or three (usually stragglers). The last day I saw them, I took a feeder out, just in case there was one that needed to feed before it headed on. I'm in a wheelchair so I had to hold the feeder, in both hands, to hang it up. Suddenly there were a dozen or more birds buzzing around me. They were so close I could feel their wings brushing my hair. Some would hover right before my face and stare at me. Then, before I could put the feeder up, they were landing on my fingers and leaning over to feed. They were there for several minutes and then, with a final buzz around me, they were gone. They were the last I saw, that fall and I believe they were a message from Mom to let me know she was all right.

Joy fills the heart.

TWO THOUSAND YEARS TOO LATE

I took a trip to Old Bethlehem and visited the manger where the Son of God was born. I wished I could have seen The Great I Am, but I was two thousand years too late.

I walked the streets of Jerusalem, imagining I could hear His voice, teaching about love and peace, forgiveness and salvation. Then, I imagined I could hear voices crying out, "Crucify Him!" I felt tears come to my eyes.

I climbed the path to the top of Golgotha's hill. There was nothing there but weeds and stones; not even the hole where His cross had stood and I felt so alone, but I was two thousand years too late.

I dropped to my knees on the cold stony ground and remembered when I had given my heart to Him, as a child. But now, so many things had happened. My parents had died. My brother was fighting, in a war zone, in danger of losing his life. I wanted so much to see my Savior's face, but I was two thousand years too late.

I knelt and wept, pouring my tears onto the cold, stony ground. I knew He loved me and one day, I would join him, but now my heart was shattered with grief and loneliness.

Then, I saw a man dressed in a robe of snowy white and glowing like the sun. His eyes were warm and gentle, his smile so sweet. He paused for a moment and then came toward me. I just knelt there, on the ground, staring up at Him. He came to me, held out His nail-scarred hands, raised me to my feet and wiped away my tears.

"There's no need to grieve, my child." He said. "Your parents are with Me. In eternity time has no meaning. Two thousand years past or two thousand more are but the wink of the eye, to eternity. I will always be with you and you with me.

He put his arm around my shoulders and we started back down the path, from Golgotha. Then, He vanished but I knew He was still with me and I realized that, as long as I believed, I would never be two late.

Eternity is forever. Believe and live for Him and you'll never be too late.

THE DAY THE ROSES CRIED

I often walked among a field of roses, crimson red and smelling so sweet. Birds sang from the treetops. Bees buzzed among the flowers, gathering pollen to make honey and here and there, I saw some small creature gathering seeds to take back to their homes. A small calico cat often followed me but never came near enough to be touched.

The roses bloomed near the foot of Golgotha and one day, while walking, I heard loud voices that led to the top of the hill. A man, bloody and bent, carried a cross and the crowd was crying, "Crucify Him! Crucify Him!"

Then, I could see his face. It was the man I had seen in the streets healing the sick, the blind, the lame and teaching the people to love their neighbor and to be kind to those in need. He was a good man! Why would they want to crucify Him?

They laid Him on the cross and hammered nails into his hands and feet. Then, they raised the cross and I saw a crown of thorns on his head, with drops of blood pouring down. Before he died, I heard Him say, "Father, forgive them, for they know not what they do."

I dropped to the ground and the little cat climbed into my lap and mewed again and again. We wept together for the death of the man they called Jesus. The birds stopped singing and the heavens darkened. I felt as if my heart would break and, when I looked up, I saw that the roses were no longer red. The ground beneath them was the color of blood and crimson drops fell from their petals. I saw that even the roses cried.

The little cat stayed with me and we often walked among the roses, but we never saw them turn red again.

When Jesus died, the whole world must have wept.

SEASONS

I love the spring, standing on the porch, watching the cattle chew the sweet, green grass while the calve romp and play like young children. It is a time God has made and a time for rejoicing. Soon, the cows will come in to be milked, and my day's work will begin.

One last cup of coffee and it's time to climb on the tractor to plow and sow. The sweetness of the overturned dirt has a smell that speaks of goodness to come; fresh corn, potatoes, sweet watermelons. It makes my mouth water, just thinking of it. My wife is planting the garden and it won't be long until we have fresh vegetables on the table, all from a patch of dirt.

It's amazing to think that God made mankind from a pinch of dirt and, of the millions that live on this planet, there are so many that forget His word and they are wondrous beings. They forget that they will, one day, return to the soil.

It's hard work and I'm tired when the day is done, but when I sit down at the table and bless the food we've grown from our own hands, we thank the Lord for all He has done.

Then, when we put the kids to bed and help them say their prayers, it's a peaceful and wonderful time.

I like the summer. You can see the crop growing; there are trees to shade you, flowers to dazzles eyes and wild plants you can harvest, to eat. When I'm not busy, the wife and kids and I get our buckets and head into the woods. You can hear someone yelling, "I got some! I got some!". We bring home wild greens, asparagus, blackberries and wild strawberries. For supper, my wife makes a cobbler and we eat like kings, all because of what God has made.

Sometimes, we go fishing and, inviting the neighbors, have a fish fry. There's just no end to the wonderful things the Lord has provided.

I like the fall. Trees are turning all kinds of colors, nuts are dropping and we pick them up by the bushel. They sure taste good. Hay's been mowed, baled and stacked to feed the cows when the weather starts getting cold. Geese are flying overhead and I can hear the music of their honking. It's time to chop and stack wood in case we have a power failure and need to stoke up a fire, in the fireplace. Dog lies in a warm spot, cat climbs into my lap. Except for milking and feeding the cows, it's a time to kind of wind down.

I like winter. Snow drifts down soft and lazy. The ground turns white. We put seeds out for the birds and then sit by the window to watch them eat. It gets cold, but we still go out for snowball fights. I enjoy it as much as the kids. Christmas approaches and we go out to cut down a tree. We spend the evening decorating it with lights and ornaments and a beautiful Angel on the top and a manger scene at the bottom to remind us of the birth of Jesus, the Son of God. Then we pack up boxes of groceries and toys for our neighbors who don't have much. It's a joy when we see the kids' faces as they find they have presents, candy and food for a good meal.

I wish the whole world thought more about others than about themselves. Maybe we'd finally have the peace and love God planned for us.

The seasons of the year are a gift from God.

DAYBREAK
A song

The first blush of dawnin', the sun starts to rise.
I hear the birds singin' as I open my eyes.
I get out of bed and go down on my knees
To thank you Lord for what you've given to me.
Joy, in the mornin', my heart and my soul,
Lord, with you beside me, it makes me feel whole.
Nothin' and no one can tear us apart.
Lord, in the mornin' you're deep in my heart.
I go down to breakfast and my dear family.
Lord, they're the gift that you've given to me.
Then, off to my job and I work really hard.
And when I get home I'm feelin' so tired
But I hug my dear children and kiss my sweet wife.
Lord, I thank you for this wonderful life.
We sit down to supper and hold hands to pray.
Lord, it's been a real blessed day.
Lord in the evenin' the moon's shinin' bright.
The kids said their prayers and they're all tucked in tight.
My wife's in my arms and it's hard to believe
You died on the cross, just to save me.
Yes, you died on that cross for my family and me.
Christ died to bring peace and joy to all.

THE STORM

I take my little ship out into the sea so I can enjoy the swish of water along her sides. Spray blows over me and I taste its salt. Seagulls cry overhead and I feel such pleasure. The sea is a beautiful azure blue and I love the look of it. Dolphins swim alongside and look up at me as if they are challenging me to race. I love those funny face little creatures and I think they like me because they always appear when I go out and challenge me to race. Suddenly, they stop and, after chattering to one another, turn and race away. I wonder why but then I understand.

There's a storm coming. I can feel it. The skies are darkening and the waves are lapping a little higher. My little ship shudders like a frightened beast. I make sure everything is battened down and then put my hands on the wheel.

It isn't strong enough yet, to be afraid, but I know it's going to get worse, much worse and I want to be ready. The wind comes up and starts to moan. I feel the power of the storm. Now I see the waves growing bigger and stronger and I grip the wheel as hard as I can. The storm strengthens and I pray." Lord, I really need your help. I've never been in a storm like this and I'm afraid. Then, I feel another pair of hands, with mine, and hear a voice that says "Don't be afraid, my child. You will weather the storm".

Huge waves grip my little ship, carrying it to the top and then plunging it down into the trough. Then another, even bigger wave grips my ship and plunges me so deep I imagine I can see the bottom of the sea, but the hands are still with me and I feel a presence behind me, but I don't look; I'm too busy fighting the storm. The wind howls like a banshee and lightning flashes so brightly, it almost blinds me. The wind howls even louder. It's like an evil voice threatening to tear my ship apart and plunge me into the center of the world. But I'm no longer afraid. I know who is with me.

Suddenly, a shudder tears me loose from the wheel and I almost fall, but the hands catch me and lift me up. I grip the wheel and fight the storm. I'm becoming exhausted, but I keep fighting. Finally, the angry storm begins to lessen and slowly, very slowly, the sea calms. A ray of sunlight breaks through the clouds and I am safe and alive. I turn and there, behind me, is a man in white who glows brighter than the sunlight. He reaches his hands out to me and I see the nail scars. He takes me in his arms and holds me. "I will always be with you when you call. With me, you will always weather the storm." He said. Then He slowly faded away. I drop to my knees and thank Him for loving me. Then I hear a voice, like a whisper. "I will always be with you to help you weather your storms.

Never fear the storms, in life; the Lord is always there to help you weather them.

STARLIGHT

Sometimes, I stand and look up at the brightness and beauty of the stars. I marvel at the wonder I see and thank the Creator of it all. I stand and stare, like a wide-eyed child, at its sheer magic. Some people wonder how such beauty was made. Scientists theorize that it was created by a big bang that scattered it all about.

I know how it was made. In a time long long ago, when the universe was almost empty, God gathered all the dust and debris into a bundle. Then he placed his hands around it, blew on it, slapped His hands together and the miracle of stars and planets, asteroids and meteors flew out to fill the empty space and He was pleased, but there was one small space He had saved for something special.

He went to that small place, gathered all the dust and debris He had caused to settle there and created a sun, a moon and a planet. But, the planet was bare and had no dimension, so he set about to change it. He created great mountains and deep valleys but left some of the land smooth and flat. Then he created trees of many shapes and colors and planted them all over the world, each in a place where they would prosper. He created plants and flowers that brought color to the planet. But he still wasn't finished.

He dug great holes, in the earth and filled them with water. The large ones He called oceans, the smaller He called seas. He created lakes and, with the tip of his finger, dug trenches that chattered and bubbled over stones, on the way from the lakes to the oceans and seas.

Next, He created animals. Some were very large, some were small. Each kind would live to the end of their time and then fade away. Others would live on and change. One, the size of a dog, would live and change to become the horse. Others would grow smaller and become otters and beavers, mice and squirrels and many other kinds of animals. Some would grow wings and learn to sing, so they filled the world with music.

God smiled, satisfied with his work. But there was one more thing to do. He went to a place he had left untouched and there He created plants that were beautiful and others that were meant to be eaten. One, in the center of the garden that He created was a tree that was forbidden for food.

Then He took a bit of dirt, spat on it and worked it into clay. Of the clay, He created a creature that had two legs with feet, two arms with hands and fingers and a head, with eyes, a nose and mouth. He looked at his creation and, taking a deep breath, blew into its nostrils and it became alive. He helped the creature to its feet and said, "You, I will call man and your name will be Adam. I have created you to be the keeper of this garden. You may eat of all the food plants, but you are forbidden to touch the tree in the center of it." He walked, with Adam, showing him the food he could eat. Then He realized that Adam would probably become lonely, so He caused him to sleep and taking a rib from him, created a woman He named Eve. Adam and Eve were God's greatest creation because it was the beginning of what we know today.

> I look up at the stars and know, in my
> heart, it was all the creation of God.

LORD, WE NEED RAIN

The fields are plowed. The seed is sown.

The weather's hot and we need rain.

Down on my knees, my body sweatin'

Head down, in prayer, 'cause we need rain.

Some people laugh and say I'm foolish

There ain't no God to make it rain.

But, I know better because He has promised

To always answer prayer. Using a hose,

I fill the stock tank and my dog Dandy

Jumps in the water for a nice cool swim.

I laugh, as he showers me with that cool water.

Then I kneel to say my prayer and Dandy's

Right there beside me, rump in the air, chin on his paws.

He knows what's important so he's prayin', too.

Then, I see my neighbors pullin' in the yard and my

Next door neighbor asked, "Mind if we join you?"

"Pick yourself a piece of dirt."

They all kneeled and we had a good prayer fest.

When they left, several were wiping away tears.

That night, in bed, my arm around my wife and her head

On my shoulder, she looked up at me and said, "Honey,

We've prayed and prayed. When is the Lord gonna bring rain?" "All in good time, Love. He knows all our needs."

Lying there, in the darkness of the night, I heard a sound; A soft pattering, on the window pane and smelled the soft, fragrance

Of damp earth. The rain had come, at last.

So, for all of you who believe that prayer is foolish I hope you enjoy the rain.

Faith and belief are the true staff of life.

CROSSING JORDAN
A song

I'm gonna' cross that river.

I'm gonna' cross that river.

I'm gonna cross that river;

The river Jordan, to the other side.

There I'll see my Savior

With a smile in His eyes.

He'll help me up from the water And He'll say
"Welcome, child. We will walk the streets of Heaven

And we'll hear the angels sing.

Then, He'll take me to the Father.

What a joy that will bring.

I'm gonna' cross that river.

I'm gonna' cross that river,

I'm gonna' cross that river;

The river Jordan, to the other side.

There I'll see my Mother.

There I'll see my Father.

There I'll see my family;

What a reunion that will be.

We will walk the fields of Heaven Where the sun always shines. There'll be no sickness, pain or sorrow Only peace and joy all the time.

So, I'm gonna' cross that river.

I'm gonna' cross that river.

I'm gonna' cross that river;

The river Jordan, to the other side.

Goin' to the glory on Heaven's side.

About the Author

My name is Pat Rogers. I'm eighty-one years old but have always had a passion for books. I wake up, in the night, with a new book, poem or song running through my head. I don't know how to write the music, but I know how the songs sound. I have so many handwritten books that I decided it was time to start getting them published. This is my third. I hope you enjoy all the people and activities in this book. I'd love to hear from my readers. Just go to patrogersbooks.com